Birds
of the
Gulf
Coast

Birds of the Gulf Coast

Photographs by
Brian K. Miller

Text by
William R. Fontenot

LOUISIANA STATE UNIVERSITY PRESS

BATON ROUGE

Manufactured in China
First printing
10   09   08   07   06   05   04   03   02   01
5   4   3   2   1

Designer: Laura Roubique Gleason
Typeface: Minion
Printer and binder: Everbest Printing Co., Hong Kong, through Four Colour
    Imports, Ltd., Louisville, Kentucky

Library of Congress Cataloging-in-Publication Data:

Miller, Brian K. (Brian Keith). 1962–
    Birds of the Gulf Coast / Brian K. Miller and William R. Fontenot.
        p. cm.
    ISBN 0-8071-2724-8 (cloth : alk. paper)
    1. Birds—Gulf Coast (U.S.)   I. Fontenot, William R.   II. Title.

    QL683.G85 2001
    598'.0976—dc21

    2001001767

But ask the beasts, and they will teach you; the birds of the air, and they will tell you;

or the plants of the earth, and they will teach you; and the fish of the sea will declare to you.

Who among all these does not know that the hand of the Lord has done this?

In his hand is the life of every living thing and the breath of all mankind.

—Job 12:7–10

Contents

Acknowledgments

We would like to thank Wylie Barrow, Van Remsen, and George Roupe for their many comments and suggestions, which resulted in a greatly improved manuscript; Lydia Daigle Fontenot for her unflagging encouragement and support over the course of this project; the many people who allowed access to their land, including Mr. and Mrs. Mike Allen, Miriam Davey, Warren Ducre, Martin Guidry, Van Remsen, Nelson Soileau, and Carmen Quebedeaux; Mark Swan for his support and expertise in locating potential subjects; Paul Conover for his technical assistance; and Steve Cardiff and Donna Dittmann for their technical support and access to their land.

Birds
of the
Gulf
Coast

Introduction

The lands adjoining the northern coast of the Gulf of Mexico include dozens of individual habitat types, from the driest shortleaf pine-oak hills to the perennially wet marshes and swamps of the coastal zone itself. Likewise, the animal communities that have developed in response to this floristic diversity are remarkably rich and complex. Lying between the temperate interior of the North American continent and the New World tropical zone of Central and South America only a few hundred miles to the south, the Gulf Coast bioregion experiences a diversity of climatic conditions that are reflected in the complexity of its flora and fauna. In addition to the pine-dominated sand and clay hills and mucky, fecund swamps and marshes, other important Gulf Coast ecosystems include beech-magnolia transition forests, broadleaf evergreen maritime forests, bottomland hardwood and other riparian forests, calcareous prairies, barrier islands, and the beaches and near-shore waters themselves. Agriculture, forestry, and petroleum exploration and production activities have had their impacts upon the Gulf Coast environment—many negative and others notably positive.

Upon this predominantly moist, sultry backdrop lives a bird community comprising three hundred or more species, depending on the season. Waders and seabirds, shorebirds and raptors, waterfowl, swifts and swallows, nightjars and owls, hummingbirds, vireos, thrushes and mimic thrushes, warblers, grosbeaks, tanagers, larks, orioles, blackbirds, sparrows, and finches all swirl in and out with the seasons. Seasonality means everything on the temperate Gulf Coast. Summer and winter bird populations are so disparate as to barely resemble one another, and the spring and fall months are punctuated by hundreds of millions of migrating avian waifs that fill the forests, grasslands, and waterways. Forming the southern terminus of the eastern half of the North American continent, the Gulf Coast acts as a crossroads for three major continental flyways and is routinely visited by "vagrant" birds from the Pacific Coast, Mexico, and the Caribbean.

We sincerely hope that this book will in some degree convey the true sense of luxuriant abundance that characterizes the bird life of the Gulf Coast region. Moreover, our greatest wish is that this book will inspire its readers to go out to woodlands, marshes, and beaches to see for themselves the avian riches that await. It is never too late to develop an authentic appreciation and empathy for what remains of our natural world and a sense of solidarity with it that will gradually transform those who experience it into backyard conservationists and citizen-scientists with a commitment to accommodating the needs of wildlife.

Male Scarlet Tanager, Lake Martin, Louisiana

Spring

*A*h, spring on the Gulf Coast. To describe the bird population at that time of year, the term "Grand Central Station" comes to mind, but in reality that term may be a bit too confining. Beginning in midwinter, Purple Martins initiate their northward trek from the tropics, reaching the U.S. Gulf Coast as early as late January. About one month later, Ruby-throated Hummingbirds, Barn Swallows, and Northern Parula and Yellow-throated Warblers follow suit. By mid-March, the avian trickle begins widening into a flow—at about the same time that local year-round Gulf Coast species (Red-bellied, Downy, and Hairy Woodpeckers; Carolina Chickadee; Tufted Titmouse; Brown Thrasher; and Northern Mockingbird, to mention a few) begin their courtship, breeding, and nesting rituals. By late April, the migratory faucet has opened up into a flood, with millions of flycatchers, vireos, warblers, tanagers, grosbeaks, orioles, buntings, and sparrows either crossing or circumnavigating the Gulf of Mexico on a daily basis. At the same time, many of the Gulf Coast's winter

Male Ruby-throated Hummingbird at banding station, Tenneco Woods, Louisiana

visitors, such as Red-tailed and Sharp-shinned Hawks; American Kestrels; Cedar Waxwings; Ruby-crowned Kinglets; American Robins; American Goldfinches; and Swamp, Song, Savannah, and White-throated Sparrows, are still soaking up food and warmth in preparation for their own treks back to northern breeding grounds.

The Mystery of Migration

At least two-thirds of the United States' bird species are long-distance migrants. Exactly what is it that drives an organism as seemingly fragile as a songbird to routinely undertake a journey as arduous and dangerous as the more than two-thousand-mile route from U.S. breeding grounds to Central and South American wintering grounds? Although debate over this issue has raged for many decades, it is now understood that the unrelenting biological drives for food and sex are what dictate when and how an organism migrates. Thus, seasonally diminishing food

Male Hooded Warbler, Sabine Woods, Texas

Male and female Eastern Bluebirds, Mary Ann Brown Preserve, Louisiana

resources drive most U.S. and Canadian birds southward toward more favorable foraging in the fall and winter, and the urge for reproduction drives them back northward during the spring months. For some birds, the fall or winter migration to more favorable foraging grounds may be as short as flying down from a mountain into the valley below. For others, the process might sweep them from breeding grounds near the Arctic Circle all the way to equatorial or even temperate South America, with many such long-distance travelers passing over the Gulf Coast each year.

How do migratory birds know where they're going—especially those younger birds who are making the journey for the first time? It is understood that the young of some bird species are escorted by one or both parents during maiden voyages, but this of course does not explain how these birds might still arrive at their respective destinations after being separated from their escorts, much less how young birds of species that do not offer escort can successfully complete their journeys. Research has shown

that birds navigate using a variety of cues. Some species use the position of the sun to guide them, constantly adjusting for the sun's changing position. Others use the position of the North Star and surrounding constellations as cues. Most recently, it has been found that several species of birds use the earth's magnetic field to tell direction, and

Gray-cheeked Thrush, Sabine Woods, Texas

it is suspected that this ability is probably widespread among birds. The vast majority of healthy migratory birds apparently know where they're going, and how to get there!

Circumgulf and Transgulf Migration

The concept of "transgulf migration" was first proposed by W. W. Cooke around the turn of the twentieth century. Apparently, little additional thought was given to it by the ornithological community until 1945, when two papers appeared almost simultaneously in two different ornithological journals. Rice University zoologist George G. Williams contended that there was plenty of evidence for *circumgulf* migration (that is, around the coastal bend of Texas), whereas virtually no evidence existed for transgulf migration. Louisiana State University zoologist George Lowery Jr., on the other hand, was the first researcher to actually document the transgulf migrational process through careful observations along the Louisiana and northwestern Florida coasts and the northern coast of the Yucatán Peninsula and aboard ships in the middle of the Gulf of Mexico.

Actually, indications of this phenomenon had been documented long before then. Among the first was a note from the journal of nineteenth-century timber surveyor John Landreth. Upon his return from a surveying trip in Louisiana and Alabama, Landreth recorded the following passage in his journal approximately forty-eight hours after his schooner, the *Non Such*, had departed Mobile Point, headed eastward in the northern Gulf of Mexico: "Saturday April 24, 1819. These 24 hours head winds with sudden squalls throughout with severe thunder and lightning and a great fall of rain. A great many birds round us . . . hawks, swallows, and other small birds. A very heavy swell . . . Lat 29.25N Long 86.43W." The date of this journal entry tells us that Landreth was traveling during the peak of spring migration on the Gulf Coast. That the entry was made during a storm also provides us with at least a preliminary notion that rain can bring a quick halt to the migrational procession, even when the procession happens to be over water.

The following excerpt from George Lowery Jr.'s *Louisiana Birds*, gives a firsthand account of the effects of rain during a transgulf migration event. The location is in Cameron Parish, on the Gulf Coast of extreme southwest-

Great Egrets, Smith Oaks Sanctuary, High Island, Texas

ern Louisiana. The date is April 24, 1953, exactly 134 years after Landreth's entry.

Shortly after midday on this particular occasion the skies became heavily overcast and the southerly winds stronger and more variable. . . . Since a norther was obviously in the offing, my companion and I immediately went to Willow Island . . . and there made a search for transients. The only migrant that we found in a small woodland covering approximately ten acres was a single Blackpoll Warbler. A few minutes later we walked into a clearing not far from the Gulf beach and glanced up at the black clouds rushing overhead. Suddenly one of us noticed a succession of dark specks against the clouds, moving in the same direction as the clouds, from south to north, hence from the direction of the open Gulf. . . . These specks, on close inspection with binoculars, proved to be hundreds of small birds. Most of the birds observed passed out of sight to the north, but not infrequently we would see one suddenly pitch downward . . . to alight in the clump of trees along the ridge. . . . After watching the spectacle from our clearing for 30 minutes or more, we could not resist investigating the changes that the descent of a portion of the overhead flight had effected in the 10-acre woodland. . . . Walking back into the wood, we discovered that the trees were teeming with birds, some trees with as many as several dozen. Despite the windy and rainy weather conditions that prevailed for the remainder of this eventful afternoon, we identified 29 species of transients, including 14 kinds of warblers.

Over time, increasing numbers of Gulf Coast birders have come to witness numerous storm-related fallout events like that described by Lowery. Indeed, even under less threatening weather conditions, selected coastal woodlands at Florida's St. George Island, St. Joseph Peninsula, St. Andrew's Island, Fort Pickens, and Gulf Breeze community; Alabama's Dauphin Island and Fort Morgan; Louisiana's Grand Isle, Pecan Island, and Peveto Beach; and Texas'

Barn Swallows, Ogden Bay Waterfowl Management Area, Utah. Common Gulf Coast breeders and migrants.

Female Black-and-white Warbler, Sabine Woods, Texas

High Island and Smith Woods are often loaded with tired, hungry birds during the month of April. During such times, a dozen or more different bird species have been counted on a single tree, and as many as twenty-two species of warblers have been recorded in a single day in woodlands of no more than a couple of acres.

The basis for such avian variety at each of these coastal woodlands is a combination of the quasi-subtropical ecology and the overall physical structure—the former of vital importance to the birds and the latter, to the bird watchers. Because of their proximity to the Gulf waters, coastal woodlands contain only plants that are able to tolerate strong, salt-laden breezes. Dominant tree species include coast live oak, hackberry, mulberry, green hawthorn, prickly ash, and honey locust. It is no small coincidence that the insect community harbored by these particular trees, and at this particular latitude, launches headlong into a massive reproductive effort at the very period in

which tired, hungry migrant songbirds stand to benefit most from the resultant eggs and larvae.

By studying the foraging habits of migratory songbirds within Gulf Coastal woodlands, bird ecologist Dr. Wylie Barrow has discovered ample evidence of this serendipitous arrangement between trees, insects, birds, and season. The tiny maggotlike larvae of the honey locust pod gall midge are deposited within equally tiny honey locust leaflets, providing nutritious "sandwiches" for Rose-breasted Grosbeaks, Blue Grosbeaks, and Indigo Buntings. Barrow has noted similar relationships with scale insect and beetle larvae outbreaks on prickly ash trees. Inchworms (the larvae of an order of small, geometrid moths) hatch out in hackberry trees, eventually dropping to the ground on silken strands when they are ready to pupate. During mass outbreaks—which occur frequently within the hackberry groves along the coast in April and May—vireos, thrushes, mimic thrushes, and warblers can be observed greedily preying upon these worms, both up in the trees, and down on the ground itself. Barrow has seen instances of such dedicated arborealists as Cerulean Warblers and American Redstarts actually shifting to ground feeding once the inchworms drop to the ground for pupation.

Because of their continuous exposure to the salt and wind, the trees of Gulf Coastal woodlands grow to only half or less of their normal mature heights, rendering these woodlands quite compact in stature. Consequently, the

Male and female Rose-breasted Grosbeaks, Sabine Woods, Texas

stunted nature of the habitat, combined with the concentrated and diverse nature of the migratory bird life, presents unparalleled viewing opportunities for birders and bird researchers alike. For those birders who have struggled for hours on end in attempts to observe canopy-level bird species such as Northern Parula, Yellow-throated, and Cerulean Warblers or Summer and Scarlet Tanagers in their typical treetop haunts are doubtlessly acquainted with the term "warbler neck." Consider, then, the possibility of viewing all five of these species at once, no more than fifteen feet up in a stunted oak or hackberry tree. Such is the allure of spring birding along the Gulf Coast.

Male Scarlet Tanager, Sabine Woods, Texas

One of this writer's first and most memorable spring birding experiences on the coast took place at the edge of a baseball field complex no more than a quarter of a mile north of the beach in the community of Cameron, Louisiana. Initially, my partner and I were attracted by a mixed flock of a few dozen Long-billed Curlew and Marbled Godwit hunting prey in one of the rain-soaked ball fields. Nearby, within a single sweet acacia bush in full bloom, sat fourteen freshly arrived male Indigo Buntings. That combination of "hot metallic" blue plumage dotted throughout a dense backdrop of bright orange, anise-scented acacia blooms remains as mentally fresh and vivid as if it had happened yesterday.

Regardless of what scientists have learned about it thus far, bird migration in general remains a mysterious and awe-inspiring topic. Even more enigmatic is the process by which a bird as small as a warbler or even a hummingbird is somehow able to fly nonstop over hundreds of miles of oceanic water to reach its migratory destination. Yet hundreds of millions of these birds accomplish this amazing feat year in and year out.

Because the bulk of transgulf migration occurs over water, it has been difficult for ornithologists to study the phenomenon *in situ,* but two recent developments have combined to shed much light on this very special avian migration route. The first involves the radar research of Clemson University ornithologist (and former George Lowery Jr. student) Dr. Sidney Gauthreaux . By using data from several radar stations along the Gulf Coast, Gauthreaux and his students have learned much concerning the timing and magnitude of avian migration over the Gulf of Mexico.

The second recent development is a project conducted by the Louisiana State University Museum of Natural Science in cooperation with the LSU Coastal Marine Institute, the U.S. Minerals Management Service, and several major oil companies that conduct exploration and production activities in the Gulf of Mexico. Established in 1998 by LSU ornithologist Van Remsen and Don Norman, the Migration Over the Gulf Project (MOGP) selects up to ten offshore oil production and/or exploration platforms per migratory season and places a seasoned ornithological observer aboard each platform. Each observer follows an established series of watches each day and compiles results on data sheets. Thus far, observers have manned ten to fifteen different offshore platforms between the coastal tip of Texas to Apalachicola Bay, Florida. As a result of these studies, much has been learned regarding not only bird migration but also the status and distribution of many species of pelagic seabirds in the Gulf of Mexico. Observers also keep data on marine mammal and insect (mostly butterfly and moth) sightings.

Among other things, MOGP observers have noted that the presence of oil production and exploration platforms in the Gulf of Mexico may well save the lives of many migrants, especially during periods of stormy weather. Consider this report from veteran Texas birder John Arvin, who was stationed aboard one of the platforms during a period of inclement weather on the night of April 29, 1998:

> Up nearly all night marveling. The river of birds continued unabated, ranging from 30–50 birds passing my position per second in the illuminated air space. . . . On my 05:00 round I found the well bay full of birds . . . the sheer numbers of Catharus thrushes was staggering. I could clearly identify Veeries flying by, and the calls of Gray-cheekeds were constant all night. . . . It is now just daylight and the flow seems to have stopped or to have gained enough altitude that I can no longer see them with the unaided eye, though there are birds flying around the platform in random directions that had evidently put down during the night and now are being stirred up by human activity. I could see many tails of sleeping birds sticking out from the beams of the ceilings on the 05:00 round.

Although MOGP work concluded in spring 2000 in the Gulf of Mexico, land-based ecological, nutritional, physiological, and other research continues to be carried out by various research entities throughout the Gulf Coastal states. Paramount to all of these studies is the designation of specific migratory "stopover habitat" areas along the coast that might be preserved and scheduled for further study. In many instances, vegetational communities within the identified traditional stopover sites have been severely compromised by livestock grazing or oil and gas exploration and production activities. At this time, both private and governmental conservation agencies are working to acquire as many of these designated resting and refueling locales as possible to ensure their future survival and that of the birds that depend upon them.

Black-bellied Plover, Port Fourchon, Louisiana

White-rumped Sandpiper, Rayne, Louisiana

Least Bittern, Anahuac National Wildlife Refuge, Texas *(left)*

Solitary Sandpiper, Lake Martin, Louisiana

Male Hooded Merganser, Knoxville, Tennessee. A common Gulf Coast breeder and year-round resident.

Long-billed Dowitcher and Stilt Sandpiper, near Lacassine, Louisiana

Dowitchers, East Jetty, south of Cameron, Louisiana

Purple Gallinule, east of Creole, Louisiana

Whimbrel, Rockport, Texas *(right)*

Black-bellied Whistling-Ducks, Rockport, Texas *(overleaf)*

Male and female Wood Ducks, Baton Rouge, Louisiana

Cattle Egret, Lake Martin, Louisiana

Little Blue Heron, Avery Island, Louisiana *(left)*

Male Boat-tailed Grackle, Sabine National Wildlife Refuge, Louisiana

Male Red-winged Blackbird, Sabine National Wildlife Refuge, Louisiana

Male Rose-breasted Grosbeak, Sabine Woods, Texas *(right)*

Male Indigo Bunting, Sabine Woods, Texas

Male Yellow-throated Vireo, Hollyman-Shealy Bird Sanctuary, Louisiana

Male Northern Parula, Barataria Preserve,
Jean Lafitte National Historic Park,
Louisiana

Chestnut-sided Warbler, Sabine Woods, Texas

Male Bay-breasted Warbler, Hollyman-Shealy Bird Sanctuary, Louisiana

Male Golden-winged Warbler, Sabine Woods, Texas

Cattle Egret in nuptial plumage, southeast
of Sorrento, Louisiana

Male Canada Warbler, Sabine Woods, Texas

Ruby-throated Hummingbird, Baton Rouge, Louisiana

Veery, Sabine Woods, Texas

Summer

The massive spring migration push along the Gulf Coast generally ends during the latter half of May. By that time, most year-round residents, such as the various woodpeckers, Tufted Titmouse, Carolina Chickadee, Northern Mockingbird, Brown Thrasher, and Northern Cardinal, have already raised and fledged their broods, making room for the newly arrived migratory tenants to get down to the business of nesting. In the insect-rich woodlands adjacent to the coast itself, nesting is surprisingly sparse, with only a few of the most adaptable species, such as White-eyed Vireo and Painted Bunting, making do within the widely mixed vegetation there.

Male Painted Bunting, south of Henderson, Louisiana

Male Baltimore Oriole, Sabine Woods, Texas

For the most part, migratory species seem more specialized in their nesting habitat preferences. Ruby-throated Hummingbirds and Orchard Orioles are partial to the wooded edges of permanent water bodies such as bayous, rivers, lakes, and swamps. Great Crested Flycatchers, Summer Tanagers, and Baltimore Orioles appreciate more open, parklike settings studded with large, mature shade trees, especially pecans. Yellow-throated and Northern Parula Warblers go for the tight clusters of Spanish moss that adorn the tops of live oaks and bald cypresses in bottomland hardwood areas. Worm-eating Warblers are magnetically attracted to the sharply undulating hills of beech-magnolia transition forests. In general, it seems that most individual birds prefer to return to the exact spot where they experienced nesting success during the previous year's breeding season. This phenomenon, known as *nesting site fidelity,* has been documented on numerous occasions and in numerous settings with data collected in bird-banding programs.

As a result of the region's high moisture and extended growing season, Gulf Coast vegetation is densely arranged, offering a plethora of both foraging and nesting sites for breeding birds. Consequently, the density of breeding and nesting individuals can be exceedingly high in many habitats. Yellow-breasted Chats crowd into the expansive blackberry patches that form an interface between millions of acres of farm and forest. Hedgelike thickets of elderberry, roughleaf dogwood, ragweed, and wild rose run for miles on end, housing all manner of nesting animals, including dozens of bird species. One of the more noteworthy examples of the

Great Blue Heron, Venice Rookery, Venice, Florida

Least Tern, Biloxi, Mississippi

productivity associated with Gulf Coast hedge thickets of this type is a system that runs for nearly two hundred miles along both the east and west protection levees of south central Louisiana's Atchafalaya Basin, the largest remaining river swamp in the nation. There, male Painted Buntings set up individual breeding territories at a rate of about five per hedge-thicket mile, indicating that approximately one thousand Painted Bunting nests are set up along the edges of this swamp alone each year (assuming that each male is able to attract at least one nesting female to his territory each season).

The massive rookeries of colonial-nesting wading birds (herons, egrets, ibises, etc.) and sea birds (gulls, terns, skimmers) rank among the most spectacular avian events to occur each summer along the Gulf Coast. At times, the array of sights and sounds associated with even a modest-sized rookery can overwhelm the uninitiated. Generally, wading birds set up rookeries within more protected or isolated swamps throughout the region. Most often, these sites are based along dense aquatic shrub borders filled with button bush or mangrove at the edges of large stands of mature bald cypress and tupelo gum trees. To discourage the efforts of egg-stealing raccoons and opossums, the birds seem to prefer confining their rookery sites to shrub thickets situated over permanent standing water—preferably water infested with alligators. Although the birds may lose an occasional nestling to the alligators below, the real nest mortality danger lies with mammalian predators, which are greatly discouraged by the presence of the alligators.

A typical Gulf Coast wading-bird rookery can encompass from two to twenty-five acres and attract a wide variety of nesting species. Some species, such as Glossy and White-faced Ibises, Tricolored Heron, Snowy Egret, and Roseate Spoonbill, seem to prefer rookery sites within the immediate vicinity of the coast itself. Others, including Anhinga, White Ibis, Black-crowned and Yellow-crowned Night Herons, Little Blue Heron, Great Egret, and Cattle Egret, willingly nest further inland. Great Blue Herons seem to shun mixed-species rookeries, preferring to set up their own breeding colonies within the deeper, more isolated parts of swamps.

Nest building usually commences as early as March, with hardier species such as Great Egret and Cattle Egret leading the way. The rush of several hundred of these

large, graceful birds as they alight, snapping dead twigs off of local shrubs and quickly launching to deposit them at individual nest sites, is an awesome thing to witness. By late April, many additional species will have set up their nests, and by the end of May, the otherworldly cacophony of begging, newly hatched nestlings can be almost startling. Both male and female parents labor throughout the daylight hours hunting and delivering food to their young. In larger rookeries containing ten thousand or more adult birds, the constant melee of incoming and departing adults provides human onlookers with the definitive "flying circus."

Although the Wood Stork's only remaining U.S. breeding turf is in the more isolated swamps of peninsular Florida and along the Atlantic Coast of Georgia and South Carolina, this species remains a major attraction each summer along the entire Gulf Coast, by way of a phenomenon common to all wading birds known as "post-breeding dispersal." Once breeding and nesting chores

White Ibises, north of Gramercy, Louisiana

Great Egrets and Roseate Spoonbills, High Island, Texas

the early 1960s, Brown Pelican reproduction abruptly ceased throughout most of the species' Gulf Coast range. The culprit was eventually identified: a family of chlorinated hydrocarbons found in pesticides such as DDT, dieldrin, and endrin. Once in the aquatic food chain, these chemicals were magnified as they moved up from plankton to fishes to top-line predators such as the Bald Eagle, Osprey, Peregrine Falcon, and Brown Pelican, causing serious malfunctions in calcium metabolism and resulting in egg shells too thin to carry their chicks to term. But by 1968, Louisiana biologists had already begun a Brown Pelican reintroduction program using birds from Florida's

have been completed, wading birds tend to disperse northward in a relatively broad pattern. Consequently, the Wood Stork, which also breeds along the Gulf Coast of Mexico in addition to its remnant southeastern U.S. colonies, tends to disperse throughout much of the U.S. Gulf Coast. Birds show up in the region as early as the first week of June and can be found foraging in wet agricultural fields and roosting in mature, quasi-isolated cypress-tupelo swamps and riparian forests throughout the summer months. Within such habitats, flocks in numbers ranging from dozens to thousands can best be viewed during the midmorning hours, when they rise upon thermals created by the sun's heat bouncing off of the earth's surface. Gradually, they wheel in upward spirals until they reach soaring altitude and move to carefully chosen foraging sites.

Among the seabird colonies along the beaches and barrier islands, the nesting and brooding scene is essentially the same as that of the waders. With the dawning of each new day, pandemonium ensues as adults rush to and fro in efforts to secure food for their young, and air traffic is often further complicated by the presence of gulls searching for opportunities to pirate off any untended eggs or chicks.

One of the biggest success stories of seabirds that breed along the Gulf Cost is that of the Brown Pelican. In

Wood Stork, Everglades National Park, Florida

Feeding Brown Pelicans, Queen Bess Island, Louisiana

Atlantic Coast colonies, which were least affected by the poisoning. After a thirty-year series of peaks and valleys, the Brown Pelican has finally regained its hold along the Gulf Coast, with fifty thousand birds censused in Louisiana alone in 1999.

Over the past several decades, the combination of hurricanes and winter storms, general coastal erosion, and increased development of beach-front properties has se-

Prothonotary Warbler, Barataria Preserve, Jean Lafitte National Historic Park, Louisiana

verely depleted the available breeding sites for gulls, terns, skimmers, and plovers, which require these sandy environs for nesting. Fortunately, state and federal wildlife agencies have experienced some success in working with local beach communities to protect traditional nesting grounds from summer beach traffic. In other instances, the birds have taken it upon themselves to seek alternative nesting habitats. For example, since the early 1990s Least Terns, Gull-billed Terns, and Black Skimmers have gradually been forming breeding colonies atop the graveled roofs of selected retail establishments throughout the New Orleans metropolitan area. Time will tell whether these new arrangements will prove suitable to both birds and humans.

By contrast, songbird nesting is a more low-key affair, where stealth replaces the "safety in numbers" strategy employed by the colonial nesters. Once breeding activities cease and nesting activities begin, male songbirds fall silent, and both parents slip quietly through the vegetation as they hunt food items for themselves and their offspring. But because of increased forest fragmentation and human development, stealth is becoming more difficult to maintain. With each passing year, more birds are being forced to nest in more marginal habitats, thus exposing their nests to more predators. Much to the delight of an equally increasing number of born-again backyard birders, a substantial number of birds such as Red-shouldered Hawk, Mississippi Kite, Mourning Dove, Eastern Screech Owl, Carolina Chickadee, Tufted Titmouse, Loggerhead Shrike, White-eyed Vireo, Prothonotary Warbler, Pine Warbler, Northern Cardinal, and Common Grackle are learning to nest in urban and suburban settings, just as the Red-bellied Woodpecker, Red-headed Woodpecker, Purple Martin, Carolina Wren, Blue Jay, American Robin, North-ern Mockingbird, Brown Thrasher, and Baltimore Oriole learned to do before them.

Fortunately, backyard birders are rapidly educating themselves on the habitat needs of nesting and wintering birds, particularly on the birds' need for water and vegetative cover. Books, CDs, Internet sites, conferences, seminars, and other programs dealing with urban and suburban wildlife gardening have mushroomed throughout the United States in recent years. As a result, unprecedented numbers of people are now involved in efforts to accommodate backyard birds.

Surveying the Situation

The North American Breeding Bird Survey (BBS) was initiated in 1966 by Chandler Robbins, one of North America's preeminent ornithologists. From the beginning, Robbins and his colleagues wanted to design a survey that could depict breeding bird populations in terms of abundance, distribution, and population trends with as much accuracy as possible. They began refining the survey techniques within the counties of Maryland and Delaware adjacent to their Patuxent Wildlife Research Center home base. Each individual survey route is 24.5 miles long, containing one stop every half mile, for a total of fifty stops per survey route. Survey participants drive the route. At each stop, birds are counted for exactly three minutes. "Countable" birds are adults (no fledglings or nestlings may be counted) that are seen or heard within a one-quarter-mile radius of the stop. Weather conditions are recorded and updated after every ten stops.

In hindsight, it is probable that not even Robbins himself could have predicted the impact that the BBS would have on present-day bird conservation efforts. Over time, the BBS has expanded to cover not only most of the United States and Canada, but also parts of Mexico and the Caribbean, involving more than 7,100 participants over the 30-year period between 1966 and 1996. Currently, there are approximately 4,100 active BBS routes in the United States and Canada, with 3,000 of these being run each year by an army of 2,500 volunteers.

Recently, BBS data from 1966 to 1996 were subjected to intense analysis. The results were mixed, showing significant population declines in about half of the four

Red-headed Woodpecker, Big Branch Marsh National Wildlife Refuge, Louisiana

Yellow-throated Warbler, Joyce Wildlife Management Area, Louisiana

to be the main culprit. The good news is that a substantial amount of wildlife management programming and conservation legislation has been enacted in the few short years since the thirty-year BBS analysis was published. Without this valuable ongoing, long-term survey, it is doubtful that wildlife managers and field ornithologists would be able to track the current status of our continent's breeding bird population.

In general, it appears that deep-woods breeders, such as the thrushes, certain warblers, and the tanagers, along with grassland breeders, which include many sparrows and other species such as some of the sandpipers, the shrikes, and the meadowlarks, are in the most trouble. Additionally, a substantial number of long-distance migratory species are feeling the effects of habitat destruction all along their migratory corridors. Presently, a strong cadre of public and private wildlife conservation agencies is working to acquire or restore crucial habitats within public lands and to educate the public about the value of individual habitat restoration efforts on private lands.

hundred bird species involved in the survey, with the remaining half either holding their own or exhibiting modest gains. Nevertheless, that half of North America's surveyed bird species are in decline is alarming news. Habitat destruction, primarily as a result of steadily increasing urbanization, agriculture, and resource extraction, appears

Eastern Meadowlark, near Kaplan, Louisiana

Mourning Dove, near Rayne, Louisiana

Carolina Chickadee, Knoxville, Tennessee. A common year-round
resident of the Gulf Coast, breeding pairs recently appearing in uban
and suburban environments.

Male Yellow Warbler, Sabine Woods, Texas *(right)*

American Swallow-tailed Kite, Lacombe, Louisiana

Mississippi Kite, Galvez, Louisiana *(left)*

Eastern Kingbird, Hollyman-
Shealy Bird Sanctuary, Louisiana

Male Northern Cardinal, High Island, Texas

Worm-eating Warbler, Sabine Pass, Texas

Prothonotary Warbler, east of
St. Francisville, Louisiana *(overleaf)*

Scissor-tailed Flycatcher, near Bell City,
Louisiana

Captive Barn Owl chicks at wildlife rehabilitator facility, Livingston, Louisiana

Red-shouldered Hawk, J. N. "Ding" Darling National Wildlife Refuge,
Florida *(right)*

Male Anhinga, Lake Martin, Louisiana

Carolina Wren, Big Branch Marsh National Wildlife Refuge,
Louisiana

Red-cockaded Woodpecker, Big Branch Marsh National Wildlife
Refuge, Louisiana

Pied-billed Grebe, west of Holly Beach, Louisiana

Mottled Duck pair, east of Creole, Louisiana

Snowy Egrets, East Jetty, south of Cameron, Louisiana

Snowy Egret, Lake Martin, Louisiana

Immature Reddish Egret, Holly Beach,
Louisiana

Immature Great Egrets, Avery Island,
Louisiana *(left)*

Green-backed Heron looking at hawk, Lake Martin, Louisiana

Laughing Gull chick, Curlew Island, Breton National Wildlife Refuge,
Louisiana *(right)*

Tricolored Heron fledglings, Avery Island, Louisiana

Great Blue Heron nesting pair, Venice
Rookery, Venice, Florida *(far right)*

Black-crowned Night-Heron, Audubon Park, New Orleans, Louisiana

White-faced Ibis, Sabine National Wildlife Refuge, Louisiana

Black Skimmers, Destin, Florida

Little Blue Herons with chicks, Avery Island, Louisiana *(left)*

Royal Tern chicks, Curlew Island, Breton National Wildlife Refuge, Louisiana

Marbled Godwit and Dowitcher, Curlew Island, Breton National Wildlife Refuge, Louisiana

Adult and young Royal Terns, Curlew Island, Breton National Wildlife Refuge, Louisiana

Sandwich Terns, Curlew Island, Breton National Wildlife Refuge, Louisiana

Purple Gallinule, Lacassine National Wildlife Refuge, Louisiana

Laughing Gulls, East Jetty, south of Cameron, Louisiana

Reddish Egret looking for fish, J. N. "Ding" Darling National Wildlife Refuge, Florida

Adult Laughing Gull, alternate plumage,
Rockport, Texas

Fall

Like spring, fall on the Gulf Coast is characterized by a large volume of migrating bird life, but the traffic is much more dispersed as species after species gradually filter down toward the Gulf of Mexico. Gone also is the harried, frenetic disposition that characterizes the spring migrants as they arrive on the coast after their nonstop northbound trips of more than six hundred miles across the Gulf. Under those circumstances, the combination of exhaustion, hunger, and thirst tends to place spring migrants in more vulnerable positions, allowing for easier viewing by birders. By contrast, fall-migrating birds are more calculating in their activities, moving about with much stealth. Thus, birding along the coast during fall migration may not be quite as spectacular in a quantitative sense. There are, however, two geographical bottlenecks or "funnels" along the coast where fall-migrating birds tend to congest: one at the northern edge of the Florida Peninsula, where it joins with the panhandle, and another at the coastal bend of Texas. In Florida, birds migrating along the eastern U.S. flyway (most of them bound for Caribbean Basin wintering grounds) must squeeze down through the peninsula as they move southward. Likewise, a substantial number of interior U.S. and Canadian birds that head for the tropics via a circumgulf route tend to crowd up along the middle and lower Texas coast as they pour in from the

Pacific Northwest, the Ohio Valley, and all points in between. Thus, Gulf Coast locations such as Tallahassee and Corpus Christi tend to host larger and more sustained volumes of bird traffic throughout the fall migration season, whereas locales in between these points tend to experience alternating waves of migrants whose movements are only somewhat dictated by the intermittent southward push of continental cool fronts.

Red-eyed Vireo, Sabine National Wildlife Refuge, Louisiana

This is not to say that Gulf Coast bird action is necessarily slow during the fall migration period. Far from it. In fact, the closer fall migrants come to the coast, the more animated their search for food becomes. To complete the trip across the Gulf of Mexico (i.e., transgulf migration), birds must nearly double their body weights. Likewise, birds that migrate around the Gulf (circumgulf migrants) must maintain a reasonable level of fat reserves to get them through the food-poor habitats that they are bound to encounter on their trip southward around the coastal bend of Texas and into Mexico. For the most part, fall food supplies throughout the United States are more plentiful than those in spring, since in addition to the usual insect and invertebrate prey, seed and berry crops will also have matured at that time. A substantial number of normally insectivorous migrants such as vireos, thrushes, tanagers, and especially the flycatchers shift the bulk of their diets to berries during fall migration.

Such a shift makes sense not only from a physical standpoint (after all, it is much easier to forage for immobile berries than for very mobile insects and invertebrates) but also from a physiological standpoint. It is fat, not protein, that affords the highest-quality fuel for long-distance traveling. Insects and other invertebrate animals contain more protein, whereas berries and other fruits contain more carbohydrates and fat. Even equipped with this understanding, though, it still nothing short of amazing to watch such dedicated insectivores as Eastern Wood Pewee, Least Flycatcher, and Red-eyed Vireo zealously guarding a prickly ash or roughleaf dogwood tree—not only for the insects that these plants might harbor, but also for their berries.

But make no mistake: by summer's end, the insect and invertebrate population along the Gulf Coast usually

Wood Thrush, Sabine Woods, Texas

mushrooms to huge proportions, so there is no shortage of biting flies, mosquitoes, grasshoppers, and other delicacies. Likewise, it is not at all unusual to observe migrant birds of many species taking advantage of these prey items. A small group of migrating Summer Tanagers may spend hours, even days, snapping up honeybees from an oak grove containing one or more hives. Southbound vireos and even Indigo and Painted Buntings will spend much time rummaging through dense stands of giant ragweed in search of the tiny geometrid moths that hide upon the undersurfaces of the leaves. Of course, gnatcatchers and warblers will be focusing much of their energies on hounding insects through local woodlands.

Still, the best places along the Gulf Coast to look for fall migrating birds are along woodland edges and agricultural hedgerows where prickly ash, roughleaf dogwood, Virginia creeper, elderberry, American beauty berry, arrowwood viburnum, and other wild berry-producers abound. Over

Philadelphia Vireo, Hollyman-Shealy Bird Sanctuary, Louisiana

the course of a fall migration season, a single tree festooned with a single Virginia creeper vine might host many hundreds of migrants. One such vine is located along a bayou fronting the Acadiana Park Nature Center in Lafayette, Louisiana (approximately fifty miles north of the Gulf Coast). Each fall, the nature center staff and its birding visitors witness amazing episodes of bird frugivory on this particular vine. Beginning at the end of August and continuing through early November, the daily parade of both local and fall-migrating birds that feed on the fruits of this vine is indeed remarkable. On certain days, especially in the month of October, the number of birds attempting to forage this particular vine results in prolonged, often chaotic "traffic jams," with birds frequently colliding as they enter and exit the all-you-can-eat buffet.

Though no quantitative data have been taken on bird usage of the Acadiana Park vine, an amazing variety of species have been observed there, including Red-bellied Woodpecker, Northern Flicker, Yellow-bellied Sapsucker, Downy Woodpecker, American Crow, Fish Crow, Wood

Thrush, Veery, Swainson's Thrush, Hermit Thrush, American Robin, Gray Catbird, Northern Mockingbird, Brown Thrasher, European Starling, White-eyed Vireo, Philadelphia Vireo, Red-eyed Vireo, Northern Cardinal, Common Grackle, Scarlet Tanager, and Summer Tanager.

The onset of fall migration along the Gulf Coast normally occurs as early as mid-July, with the appearance of Spotted Sandpiper, Least Flycatcher, Yellow Warbler, and Louisiana Waterthrush. Like the others that will follow, these "early bird" species move in silently, hugging the banks of rivers and bayous as they make their way southward. As July wears into August, the migrating sandpiper contingent swells with the addition of Pectoral Sandpiper, Long-billed Dowitcher, Lesser Yellowlegs, and Least Sandpiper. Substantial numbers of Blue-gray Gnatcatchers and Orchard Orioles also begin to filter down through riparian corridor forests. Mid-August through mid-September is flycatcher season along the Gulf Coast, as the bulk of North America's migratory flycatcher species move through the region during this period. As previously men-

Northern Waterthrush, Sabine Woods, Texas

tioned, the Gulf Coast flycatcher parade is heralded by the appearance of the Yellow-bellied, but not far behind is the Olive-sided Flycatcher, the swiftest and most powerful of the family—and also the most uncommonly observed. Olive-sideds move in small numbers, mainly through the northwestern Gulf Coast. Perhaps it is their superficial resemblance to Purple Martins (slender, but long-winged and "big-shouldered") that allows them to slip through the region mostly undetected. Louisiana and Texas Gulf Coast birders should look for Olive-sided Flycatchers at the tips of dead trees along the shores of coastal marshes, swamps, and lakes in mid to late August.

By late August, the numbers of *Empidonax* flycatchers and Eastern Wood Pewees can become nearly overwhelming within coastal woodlands. Because they are most easily identified by voice, the visually confusing "empids" can present quite an identification challenge, since they are mostly silent during fall migration. Still, there are times when they become vocal, particularly when they cluster around berry trees and begin competing for food.

Another interesting August phenomenon along the Gulf Coast is the substantial buildup of both Black and Gull-billed Terns, which are most often seen congregating

American Crow, Everglades National Park, Florida

over freshwater marshes above the coast. Occasionally, groups of over one hundred of either or both species can provide quite a spectacle as they chase schools of small fish at the marsh surfaces.

By early September, huge numbers of Blue Grosbeaks, Painted Buntings, and reclusive Mourning Warblers build up within the herbaceous thickets that line the coast. Most often, these thickets are so dense that the only sign of the activity within them is the constant calls of the well-concealed birds. Only by dropping to hands and knees and peeking through beneath the thicket can one observe the magnitude of frenzied feeding occurring within.

Throughout the month of September, migrating sandpiper, warbler, tanager, and oriole numbers steadily increase. By October, the thrushes and mimic thrushes push through, cleaning out the last of the late-summer berry crop in the process. Like the flycatchers, Gray Catbirds and Brown Thrashers are particularly fond of roughleaf dogwood fruits. By the middle of that month, it becomes very difficult to find a single roughleaf dogwood berry anywhere within the coastal zone.

With the arrival of majestic hordes of migratory ducks and geese still a month away, it is the movement of raptors—falcons, hawks, and Ospreys—that provides the most spectacular early October views along the Gulf Coast. Being mostly circumgulf migrants, these birds first follow coastal-plain bayous and rivers down to the coast itself. From there, some funnel eastward to the Florida Peninsula, but most turn westward to the bottleneck along the

Osprey, Pascagoula Naval Station, Mississippi

upper Texas coast. Spending their nights in the treetops of mature riparian forests and other coastal woodlands, mixed hawk flocks numbering from a few hundred to a few thousand individuals create memorable scenes as they rise on midmorning thermals, wheeling and spiraling upward in massive "kettle" formations before reaching soaring altitude, where, one by one, they burst off suddenly, as if shot by a cannon, toward their next dusk destinations.

In terms of species diversity, fall migration peaks along the Gulf Coast in late October. By then, well over one hundred million birds will have raked through the region's woodlands, marshes, and swamps en route to their tropical wintering grounds. Their absence, however, will not be felt for long, for even as the migrants are still departing, the winter birds are piling in.

Female Painted Bunting, Sabine Woods, Texas

Gray Catbird, Sabine Woods, Texas

White-eyed Vireo, Sabine Woods, Texas

Female Summer Tanager, Hollyman-Shealy Bird Sanctuary, Louisiana

Male and female Blue Grosbeaks, Sabine Woods, Texas *(left)*

Dickcissel, near Lacassine, Louisiana

Female Rose-breasted Grosbeak, Hollyman-Shealy Sanctuary,
Louisiana *(right)*

Belted Kingfisher, Sabine National Wildlife Refuge, Louisiana

Magnolia Warbler, Sabine Woods, Texas

Northern Rough-winged Swallows, west of Butte La Rose, Louisiana

Common Moorhen, Brazos Bend State Park, Texas

Male Blue-winged Teal, Knoxville, Tennessee. A common spring migrant and sporadic breeder in the Gulf Coast region.

Lesser Yellowlegs, Sabine National Wildlife Refuge, Louisiana

Blue-winged Teals, Cameron Parish, Louisiana *(overleaf)*

Roseate Spoonbill, Sabine National Wildlife Refuge, Louisiana

White Ibises, Alligator Bayou, Louisiana

Pectoral Sandpiper, Harold S. Crane Waterfowl Management Area, Utah. A common migrant through the Gulf Coast region.

Black Terns, Curlew Island, Breton National Wildlife Refuge, Louisiana

Sandwich Tern, Curlew Island, Breton National
Wildlife Refuge, Louisiana *(right)*

Upland Sandpiper, west of Bell City, Louisiana

Juvenile Turkey Vultures, Avery Island, Louisiana

Yellow-billed Cuckoo, Sabine Woods, Texas

Black-throated Green Warbler, Hollyman-Shealy Bird Sanctuary, Louisiana

Blue-gray Gnatcatcher, Corkscrew Swamp Sanctuary, Florida

Eastern Wood Pewee, Sabine Woods, Texas

Great Crested Flycatcher, Corkscrew Swamp Sanctuary, Florida

Male Prairie Warbler, Hollyman-Shealy Bird Sanctuary, Louisiana

Winter

Winter on the Gulf Coast, unlike in much of the United States, is a time of exuberant superabundance. During this time of the year, many species of birds become gregarious, forming large single- or mixed-species foraging flocks. Gulls and terns huddle together by the hundreds, ducks and geese by the tens of thousands, and blackbirds by the hundreds of thousands, if not millions.

American Goldfinch, west of Holly Beach, Louisiana

Throughout the marshes, swamps, and agricultural lands of the lower South, dawn and dusk of each winter day are signaled by a cacophony of cries as these flocks venture between roosting and foraging sites. American Robins, Cedar Waxwings, Eastern Bluebirds, Hermit Thrushes, and others settle into the woodlands in search of berries. Two dozen species of sparrows and finches, most of which have migrated in from the north, share these woodland fruits, along with grassland seeds of goldenrods, asters, coneflowers, and the grasses themselves—all of which they sedately munch under the retreating sun of each winter-shortened day.

As the crop of hackberry, hawthorn, and honeysuckle fruits begins to dwindle, the robins hop over to nearby close-mowed parks, ball fields, and lawns in search of earthworms. Finally, at winter's end, they rejoin the Cedar Waxwings in a massive late-season assault on wild and domestic holly berries.

Great airborne funnels of geese and blackbirds barrel across the harvested grain fields, shifting by the hour, like the rising and falling of clouds. Single flocks numbering

Swamp Sparrow, Sabine National Wildlife Refuge, Louisiana

American White Pelicans, Bolivar Flats, Texas

up to one hundred thousand geese and three hundred thousand blackbirds have been tallied over some of the richer agricultural lands. Some of these flocks are "pure" in composition, but most are mixed. Snow Geese typically compose the bulk of mixed goose flocks, joined by lesser numbers of Greater White-fronted, Ross's, and Canada Geese. Similarly, Red-winged Blackbirds make up the majority of mixed blackbird flocks, complemented with varying fractions of European Starling, Common Grackle, Brown-headed Cowbird, Brewer's Blackbird, and Rusty Blackbird.

Mallard, Northern Pintail, Northern Shoveler, Green-winged Teal, American Wigeon, and other puddle ducks eagerly join with herons, egrets, ibises, and sandpipers in scouring shallow wetlands and flooded agricultural fields for food. Out in the deeper waters of bayous, rivers, lakes, and along the near-shore waters of the Gulf itself, flocks of pelicans, skimmers, gulls, and terns mingle with huge rafts of Red-breasted Mergansers, Ring-necked Ducks, Lesser Scaup, Bufflehead, scoters, and other diving ducks.

There, where wave meets sand, one of the most breathtaking winter sights is of American White Pelicans lumbering from marsh to Gulf for roosting and feeding. Early morning flocks of a few dozen to a few hundred individuals stretch out into long flight lines, each bird perfectly spaced from his fellows, often flying no more than fifty feet above spellbound observers. Somehow, these mammoth birds (five feet in total length, with nine-foot wingspans) literally float atop the uplifting puff of air that results from the motion of the waves striking the beach. Thus fixed, they are able to remain nearly motionless, necks tucked and wings outspread, as they majestically cruise so near to the ground and so slowly that even their eyes may be leisurely studied in intimate detail.

Despite the relative rawness of the weather, winter is indeed a time of ease and plenty for these birds, temporarily freed from their nesting and migration duties. Like bus drivers and factory workers on vacation, winter birds milk the Gulf Coast for all it's worth.

Amid all of this freewheeling gregariousness, several

notable bird species find it necessary to get down to the business of breeding, nesting, and brooding their young along the Gulf Coast each winter. The southern Bald Eagle, a subspecific form of Bald Eagle, departs its northern summering grounds by fall, arriving along the Gulf Coast in late October or November. Birds pair up almost as soon as they reach the region, normally selecting nesting sites within isolated cypress-tupelo gum swamps. Young are hatched by mid to late winter and usually fledge by early spring. By late spring, both adults and young gradually begin making their way to the north—most often by way of larger rivers—where they will spend the summer around the Great Lakes.

Most year-round Gulf Coast owl species such as Great Horned, Barred, and Eastern Screech also initiate reproductive chores by midwinter. The ghoulish prebreeding vo-calizations of Barred Owls shake the clear, crisp nights of November. Young Great Horned Owl nestlings are occasionally reported as early as the Christmas Bird Count season (mid-December through the first week of January). By February, Muppet-like Eastern Screech Owl nestlings can sometimes be seen crowding the entrances of their nest cavities trying to soak up a little late-winter sun and to peer at the brand new world outside.

Neotropic versus Nearctic Migrants

Not so very long ago, all North American ornithologists referred to those birds that migrated into the tropics for winter as "neotropic" migrants and those that stopped along the U.S. Gulf Coast for winter as "nearctic" migrants. Over time, however, biologists have come to better understand the situation: for many U.S. migratory bird species, this either/or classification is largely inaccurate. Instead, these species find their winter homes along a continuum stretching from the Gulf Coastal Plain southward through Mexico and Central America. Take for example the case of the Yellow-rumped Warbler. This species commonly breeds throughout Canada, Alaska, and down into the New England, Great Lakes, and Great Basin regions of the United States. During the winter months, the Yellow-rumped Warbler makes its way southward and is a ubiquitous resident throughout the southern one-third of the United States. But the same warbler also commonly winters throughout most of Mexico, Central America, and the Greater Antilles.

This wintering continuum pattern holds true, to a lesser or greater extent, for a surprisingly large number of birds. For species such as Cedar Waxwing, Orange-

Great Horned Owl chicks, Bluebonnet Swamp, Baton Rouge, Louisiana

crowned Warbler, Yellow-rumped Warbler, Common Yellowthroat, and Grasshopper Sparrow, numbers are fairly evenly distributed between the tropical Americas and the quasi-temperate Gulf Coast. Of others, such as Tricolored Heron, Sandwich Tern, Least Flycatcher, Black-and-white Warbler, Nashville Warbler, Dickcissel, Painted and Indigo Buntings, and Clay-colored Sparrow, the vast majority are distributed within the tropics during winter, with only the northernmost edge of the wintering population being found along the Gulf Coast. Those few that remain stateside are often referred to as "lingerers" by U.S. ornithologists and birders, for whom spotting a winter "lingerer" is almost as exciting as finding a bona fide "vagrant" species.

"Vagrants" are birds that, for any number of reasons, turn up out of place, creating much excitement within the local birding communities in which they are discovered. Although vagrant species can and do appear at almost any time of the year, it seems that more cases occur along the Gulf Coast during the winter months. In recent years, some of the rarest Gulf Coast winter vagrants (known as "accidentals," seen no more than about five times per one hundred years) have included Northern Wheatear, Ferruginous Hawk, Black Brant, Tundra Swan, Sage Thrasher, and Painted Redstart. Seen on a somewhat more regular basis, approximately one to three times every five to ten

Caspian Terns and Royal Tern, Padre Island National Seashore, Texas

years, are Ruff, Townsend's Warbler, Black-throated Gray Warbler, and Green-tailed Towhee.

And then there is a group of very curious cases involving a substantial number of birds from the southwestern United States and Mexico that find their way to the Gulf Coast each winter far too regularly to be considered "vagrant" or "casual" anymore. For example, Cinnamon Teal, Groove-billed Ani, Buff-bellied Hummingbird, Ash-throated Flycatcher, and Vermilion Flycatcher are all currently considered rare but regular winter visitors, especially along the north central and western Gulf Coast. This phenomenon begs the question, Why would a bird that either commonly winters in Mexico or lives in Mexico year-round move *northeastward* during the winter? Theories that might answer this question are still being formulated. Some attribute their appearance to seasonally diminishing food or habitat resources in these birds' traditional wintering grounds. Some feel that these

Brants, Rathrevor Beach Provincail Park, Vancouver Island, British Columbia. Very rare vagrants along the Gulf Coast.

birds might possess genetic defects that send them the wrong way for winter. Others stubbornly hold on to the belief that these birds are accidentally deposited outside of their normal winter ranges by the whims of weather patterns.

Yet another peculiar winter bird phenomenon in the Gulf Coast area is the regular presence of a host of western hummingbird species each year. In addition to the Buff-bellied Hummingbird, which breeds primarily in Mexico, Rufous and Black-chinned Hummingbirds are now considered rare to uncommon—but definitely regular—winter visitors all along the Interstate-10 corridor between Houston and Pensacola. Even though all of these hummers are dedicated tropical winterers, in the winter of 1999–2000, nearly four hundred of these birds were reported from the backyards of southern Louisiana alone. In addition, several Anna's, Broad-tailed, Calliope, and Allen's Hummingbirds are recorded in this "winter hummer belt" every one to three winters, and Broad-billed and Blue-throated Hummingbirds have both been recorded in the area on several occasions in the past ten years.

Why would a bird abandon its tropical wintering turf and opt to spend those cold months in a region where safe temperatures and food supplies are iffy at best? Again, conjecture runs high on this subject within the ornithological community. Theories involving everything from genetic dysfunction to seasonally diminishing resources on traditional wintering grounds, global warming, and increased gardening for birds have been offered. At this point, however, no studies have been designed or executed to begin resolving the issue.

The fact remains that southwestern and Mexican species are finding their way to the Gulf Coast with increasing frequency during the winter months and in certain cases during the breeding and nesting season as well, most notably the White-tailed Kite (successful), Crested Caracara (probably successful), White-winged Dove (successful), Inca Dove (successful), Great Kiskadee, Couch's Kingbird, Western Kingbird (probably successful), and Yel-

White-tailed Kite, Brazoria National Wildlife Refuge, Texas

low-green Vireo. Similarly, at least two Caribbean species—Gray Kingbird and Black-whiskered Vireo—have also recently achieved sporadic breeding success on the Gulf Coast. Although the implications of such behaviors have yet to be clarified, these avian surprises are furnishing much excitement, along with healthy doses of concern, to ornithologists and amateur birders alike.

Christmas Bird Counts: Pageantry, Celebration, and Science

Initiated at the turn of the twentieth century by New England ornithologist Frank Chapman, the Christmas Bird Count was originally designed as an alternative to the rather hideous regional practice of that era in which groups of men would set out on Christmas Day and shoot

White Ibises, Sorrento, Louisiana

every bird they encountered. Over time, the Christmas Bird Count concept has spread throughout the United States, Canada, the Caribbean, portions of Latin America, and even a few Pacific Islands and has evolved into an annual celebration of winter bird life, the results of which hold a substantial degree of scientific value, particularly when the data derived are properly compared and analyzed.

Anyone can initiate or participate in a Christmas Bird Count by contacting the National Audubon Society and following a few simple rules. The count must be run on a day falling between a set of dates established by the Audubon Society. Roughly, these dates fall from about a week before through about a week after Christmas Day each year. The coordinators, or "compilers," of each local count must prescribe a fifteen-mile-diameter count circle in which the participants of that count will work. The count circle must not overlap with any other active count circle. An unlimited number of participants may sign up for any given count. Generally, the count circle is divided into sections, and the participants are divided into parties that work a predetermined section of the circle. Each team counts every bird that it sees or hears in its section. Offi-

cially, the hours for each count run from midnight to midnight of the prescribed day, but even the most ardent participants work from no more than an hour or two before dawn through about an hour or two after dusk. Each team turns in a tally sheet listing the species and numbers of birds that it encounters on count day. Data from the tally sheets are combined into final count results and forwarded for processing by the National Audubon Society.

Beyond the comradery and fun associated with a mid-winter day of birding with old and new friends, individual Christmas Bird Counts serve as important winter bird survey tools that provide a rough snapshot of winter bird life in their respective areas. Taken together, the more than two thousand counts that are currently run each year reveal continent-wide, if not hemisphere-wide, seasonal trends that would not be logistically feasible if attempted by professional ornithologists alone, particularly on an ongoing, year-by-year and decade-by-decade basis.

The level of Christmas Bird Count participation along the Gulf Coast has traditionally been stable and adequate to provide a valuable collection of bird data each year. For example, Christmas Bird Counts have tracked the Gulf Coast winter hummingbird phenomenon for years. Other important data extracted each year from Gulf Coast Christmas Bird Counts include winter waterfowl and other game bird numbers, as well as the rates at which "lingering" species are found and the frequencies of such discoveries from year to year.

Shorebird Spectacle

Although it is true that sandpipers and other shorebirds pour through the Gulf Coast in great volume during spring and fall migration, the winter months actually provide the best opportunities for long-term study of many species. As a group, shorebirds are difficult to satisfactorily observe for most American bird lovers. The primary reason for this is that most shorebird species nest in extremely isolated wilderness areas, mostly near the Arctic Circle. Once nesting chores are completed, shorebirds waste no time in racing southward to their wintering grounds. Fortunately for Gulf Coast birders, roughly half of the more than forty North American shorebird species winter as far north as the Gulf Coastal Plain.

Coastal beaches; tidal and interior marsh mud flats; wet agricultural fields; lake, river, and bayou shores; and even municipal wastewater treatment facilities are all excellent places to view and study shorebirds. During the winter months, mixed shorebird flocks often crowd into these habitats for roosting, foraging, and resting. Species such as American Oystercatcher; Piping, Snowy, Semipalmated, and Wilson's Plovers; Long-billed Curlew, Marbled Godwit; Willet; Short-billed Dowitcher; Ruddy Turnstone; and Sanderling are generally restricted to the beaches and tidal flats. Least Sandpiper, Long-billed Dowitcher, Greater and Lesser Yellowlegs, and Common Snipe tend to be found in muddy agricultural fields and mud flats within the interior marshes, and Western Sandpiper, Stilt Sandpiper (along the western part of the region), Spotted Sandpiper, American Avocet, Black-necked Stilt, Black-bellied Plover, Dunlin, and Killdeer can and do show up in any number of moist to wet habitats.

One interesting caveat regarding winter shorebird life along the Gulf Coast is that these birds are all wearing their somber (nonbreeding) plumage at that time. The plumage of almost all winter shorebird species consists of dull brown-gray or gray-brown upperparts and dingy white underparts. Thus, attempting to identify any winter shorebird by plumage alone will quickly prove frustrating, and Gulf Coast winter shorebird afficionados must learn the species based on posture, bill shape, voice, and other non-plumage-related characteristics. Out of necessity, Gulf Coast birders tend to become excellent shorebird identifiers year-round!

Marbled Godwits, Rockport, Texas

Male Pileated Woodpecker, Great Smoky Mountains National Park, Tennessee. A crow-sized common year-round resident of the Gulf Coast region.

Savannah Sparrow, south of Baton Rouge, Louisiana

Henslow's Sparrow, Lake Ramsey Wetland Preserve, Louisiana

White-crowned Sparrows, Sabine National Wildlife Refuge, Louisiana

White-throated Sparrow, Sabine Woods,
Texas *(right)*

Palm Warbler, Everglades National Park,
Florida

Male House Finch, Knoxville, Tennessee. A year-round resident of the Gulf Coast region since the 1990s.

Rufous Hummingbird, Baton Rouge, Louisiana

Broad-tailed Hummingbird, south of Baton Rouge, Louisiana

American Robin, west of Bains, Louisiana

Black-chinned Hummingbird,
Baton Rouge, Louisiana

Yellow-rumped Warblers, J. N. "Ding" Darling National Wildlife
Refuge, Florida *(right)*

Solitary Vireo, Sabine Woods, Texas

Female Northern Cardinal, Knoxville, Tennessee *(left)*. An abundant
year-round resident of the Gulf Coast region.

Captive Southern Bald Eagle, Grandfather Mountain, North Carolina. A winter nester in the Gulf Coast region, once endangered but increasing in number.

Sedge Wren, Sabine National Wildlife Refuge, Louisiana

Captive Barred Owl, Homosassa Springs State Wildlife Park, Florida (*left*)

Cedar Waxwings, Hollyman-Shealy Bird Sanctuary, Louisiana

Sora, Sabine National Wildlife Refuge, Louisiana

Common Snipe, west of Holly Beach, Louisiana

Wintering waterfowl, Sabine National Wildlife Refuge,
Louisiana *(overleaf)*

Redhead, Baton Rouge, Louisiana

Male Canvasback, Rockport, Texas

Male Mallard, Baton Rouge, Louisiana

Barred Owl, Corkscrew Swamp Sanctuary,
Florida

Snow Geese, Sabine National Wildlife Refuge, Louisiana

Greater White-fronted Geese, Pintail Wildlife Drive, Cameron Prairie National Wildlife Refuge, Louisiana

Snow Geese, near Aransas National Wildlife Refuge, Texas *(overleaf)*

Reddish Egret, Bolivar Flats, Texas

Neotropic Cormorant, Sabine National Wildlife Refuge, Louisiana *(left)*

Mississippi Sandhill Cranes, Sandhill Crane National Wildlife Refuge, Mississippi

Black-necked Stilt, near Rayne, Louisiana

Whooping Cranes, Aransas National Wildlife Refuge, Texas

Willet, Rockport, Texas

Double-crested Cormorant, Shark Valley, Everglades National Park,
Florida *(left)*

Immature Reddish Egret, Holly Beach, Louisiana

Great-tailed Grackles, Rockport, Texas

American Coots, Brazos Bend State Park, Texas

Herring Gulls, near Ucluelet, British Columbia, Canada. Common migrants, winter residents, and spring breeders along the Gulf Coast.

Semipalmated Plover, Gulfport, Mississippi

Greater and Lesser Yellowlegs, Harold S. Crane Wildlife Management Area, Utah. Among the most common shorebirds along the Gulf Coast from August to April.

American Avocets, south of Cameron, Louisiana

American White Pelican, Rockport, Texas

Long-billed Curlew, Padre Island National Seashore, Texas

Ruddy Turnstones and Sanderlings, Port Fourchon, Louisiana

Marbled Godwits, Rockport, Texas

Sanderling, Padre Island National Seashore, Texas

Laughing Gulls, Bolivar Flats, Texas

Index